North Pole, South Pole

THIS EDITION
Editorial Management by Oriel Square
Produced for DK by WonderLab Group LLC
Jennifer Emmett, Erica Green, Kate Hale, *Founders*

Editors Grace Hill Smith, Libby Romero, Maya Myers Michaela Weglinski;
Photography Editors Kelley Miller, Annette Kiesow, Nicole DiMella; **Managing Editor** Rachel Houghton;
Designers Project Design Company; **Researcher** Michelle Harris; **Copy Editor** Lori Merritt;
Indexer Connie Binder; **Proofreader** Larry Shea; **Reading Specialist** Dr. Jennifer Albro;
Curriculum Specialist Elaine Larson

Published in the United States by DK Publishing
1745 Broadway, 20th Floor, New York, NY 10019

Copyright © 2023 Dorling Kindersley Limited
DK, a Division of Penguin Random House LLC
23 24 25 26 10 9 8 7 6 5 4 3 2 1
001-333875-Oct/2023

A catalog record for this book
is available from the Library of Congress.
HC ISBN: 978-0-7440-7154-2
PB ISBN: 978-0-7440-7157-3

DK books are available at special discounts when purchased in bulk for sales promotions, premiums,
fundraising, or educational use. For details, contact: DK Publishing Special Markets,
1745 Broadway, 20th Floor, New York, NY 10019
SpecialSales@dk.com

Printed and bound in China

The publisher would like to thank the following for their kind permission to reproduce their images:
a=above; c=center; b=below; l=left; r=right; t=top; b/g=background

123RF.com: Witold Kaszkin 1b; **Alamy Stock Photo:** Flip Nicklin / Minden Pictures 17b, Kelvin Aitken / VWPics 16–17;
Depositphotos Inc: mzphoto 24br; **Dreamstime.com:** Biletskiy 4–5, Aleksandr Frolov 19br, Peter Hermes Furian 10cb,
Kira Kaplinski 9b, Yongyut Kumsri 8, Loopall 11cb, Helen Panphilova / Gazprom 3b, Gueret Pascale 21br, Angela Perryman 23bl,
Alexey Sedov 24cl, Vladimir Seliverstov 26–27, Graeme Snow 18b, Staphy 12–13, Tenedos 27cb, Christopher Wood / Chriswood44
6–7; **Getty Images:** Monica Bertolazzi 28–29, Corbis Documentary / Roger Tidman 18cr, Corbis Documentary / Staffan Widstrand
14–15, Gallo Images ROOTS RF collection / Danita Delimont 22–23, Stone / Arctic-Images 19tr, Stone / Paul Souders 23cr, 27cra;
Getty Images / iStock: E+ / ekvals 20–21, E+ / sethakan 24–25; **Shutterstock.com:** Goinyk Production 10–11

Cover images: *Front:* **Dreamstime.com:** Steve Allen / Mrallen b, Outdoorsman t

All other images © Dorling Kindersley
For more information see: www.dkimages.com

For the curious
www.dk.com

North Pole, South Pole

Jen Szymanski

DK

Contents

Ends of the Earth

The North Pole is at the very top of our planet. It is the farthest place north anyone can go. The South Pole is at the opposite end of Earth. It is the farthest point south.

The poles have two of the coldest climates on Earth. They are covered in ice, and they can be dark—or light— all day. Have you ever wondered why?

Circling the Poles

Maps and globes show a large circle around each pole. The circle around the North Pole is called the Arctic Circle. The circle around the South Pole is called the Antarctic Circle.

North Pole

Arctic Circle

Antarctic Circle

South Pole

Earth is tilted. This causes one pole to point away from the Sun during some parts of the year. In these months, the days are long and dark. It is winter, and the Sun never rises at that pole.

Polar Light Shows

Sometimes, particles from the Sun interact with Earth's upper atmosphere. This creates spectacular light shows in the sky. These displays are called the Northern and Southern Lights.

But on the other side of Earth, the opposite pole is pointing toward the Sun. It is summer. The Sun rises and then stays low in the sky all day and night. The Sun never sets!

Sunlight shines straight on Earth's middle, around the equator. The equator is very hot. But because of Earth's tilt, sunlight hits the poles at an angle. The poles do not get very much sunlight.

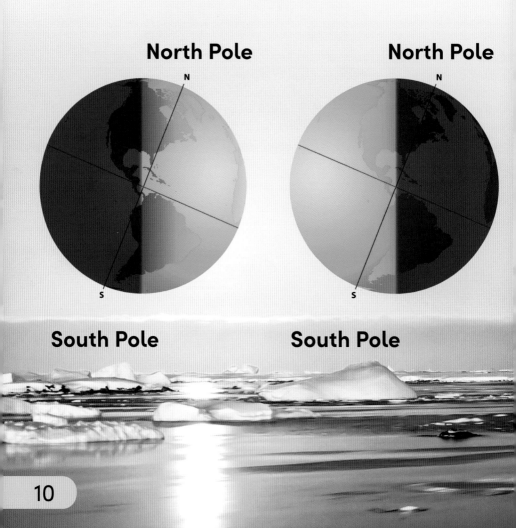

North Pole

N

S

South Pole

North Pole

N

S

South Pole

The light that does reach them is not very warm or bright. So, temperatures at the poles are very cold.

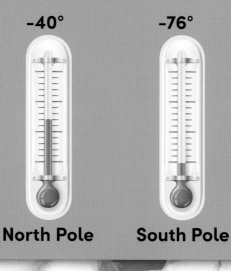

Cold and Colder

Temperatures at the North Pole drop to -40°F (-40°C) in the winter. The South Pole is much colder. There, it is -76°F (-60°C) on average in the winter! BRRR!

-40°   -76°

North Pole   South Pole

Not much rain or snow falls at Earth's poles. The climate at the poles is actually drier than some of Earth's hot, sandy deserts. So, how is it possible that the poles are covered in ice?

The cold temperatures at the poles have prevented much of the snow and ice from melting. The oldest ice near the North Pole is more than 100,000 years old. The oldest ice around the South Pole is about a million years old!

Life at the North Pole

The North Pole itself is covered by the Arctic Ocean. There is no land there at all—just water and ice. There is land around the North Pole. It is a type of ground called tundra. It is flat, treeless, and frozen.

People live at the edges of the Arctic Ocean. Some groups of people have lived there for thousands of years. People live on the tundra, too.

Many kinds of animals live around the North Pole. Some animals swim in the Arctic Ocean.

Bowhead whales stay all year. Their bodies have a thick layer of fat called blubber to keep them warm.

Narwhals live in the Arctic Ocean, too. They have a large, spiral-shaped tooth, called a tusk. This is why narwhals are called unicorns of the sea.

narwhal

Tiny animals called krill also live in the Arctic Ocean. They are food for bowhead whales and other animals. Many krill swim together. Animals swim through the krill with their mouths open to scoop up a meal.

krill

Algae float near the top of the ocean. They use light from the Sun like plants do to make their own food. Many Arctic animals eat the algae that grows in the chilly water.

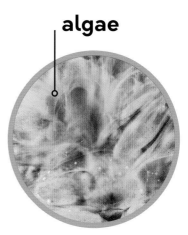

algae

Tundra Plants

Lots of plants grow on the tundra. Most of these plants don't grow to be very tall. Many have flowers, and some make fruit. These plants are food for hares, reindeer, and other animals.

The Arctic Ocean is small, and its waves don't get very big. The top layer of water freezes into ice for most of the year. Animals such as walruses rest on the ice. Seals swim in the ocean. Their fur keeps them warm and helps them glide through the water.

Polar bears live on land and walk across the ice. They are excellent swimmers. They are patient hunters, too. Polar bears often sit beside holes in the ice. They wait for a seal to pop up for a breath of air.

Arctic Adaptations

Polar bears have furry, webbed feet. The fur keeps their feet warm on the ice. The webbing helps them swim.

Life at the South Pole

The South Pole is located on land. It is part of the continent Antarctica. Antarctica has long, flat plains and high mountains.

Very few flowering plants can survive around the South Pole. But there are lots of mosses and lichen. Lichen are organisms that are part fungus and part algae.

lichen

moss

Many animals live near the South Pole. Seagulls and other birds fly low over the water near the shore. They drop down to the beach to grab tasty crabs to eat.

The birds share the beach with elephant seals. These giant animals doze in the sun. When they go for a swim, they keep a close watch out for orcas. Orcas are smart hunters that live in the ocean waters.

Emperor penguins spend their entire lives on Antarctica's ice and in the ocean. Several other kinds of penguins live here, too.

Gentoo penguins jet quickly underwater and then launch themselves onto the land. Adélie penguins are brave. They dive off icy cliffs into the water.

SPLASH!

Learning About Antarctica

No humans live full-time on Antarctica, but scientists do go there to live and work. Some scientists study the land and its plants and animals. Others sail on ships, studying the water.

Earth's poles are extreme environments, but they are full of beauty and life. They are home to many different kinds of plants and animals.

They are places to make
exciting new discoveries.

Glossary

Algae
Tiny plant-like living things that use energy from sunlight to make their own food

Antarctic Circle
A line that goes around Earth near the South Pole

Arctic Circle
A line that goes around Earth near the North Pole

Blubber
A thick layer of fat that helps some animals to stay warm

Climate
The weather a place has over a long period of time

Continent
A large area of land separated from others by water, mountains, rivers, or other natural boundaries

Equator
An imaginary line around Earth's middle that divides it into a top and bottom half

Krill
Small shrimp-like animals that live in Earth's oceans

Lichen
A living thing made when fungus and algae live together

Mosses
Small low-growing plants that often live in shady, damp places

Tundra
A treeless plain in Arctic regions with permanently frozen ground beneath the surface

Tusk
A very long tooth that can be seen even when an animal's mouth is closed

Index

Quiz

Answer the questions to see what you have learned. Check your answers in the key below.

1. Why are Earth's poles sometimes dark or light all day?

2. Which pole is covered by the Arctic Ocean?

3. What keeps bowhead whales warm as they swim in chilly waters?

4. Where is the South Pole located?

5. What are the three kinds of penguins that live around the South Pole?

1. Earth is tilted 2. The North Pole 3. A thick layer of fat called blubber 4. On the continent of Antarctica 5. Emperor, gentoo, and Adélie penguins